Place and Space
Landscapes in art

by Leo Thomson

HODDER
Wayland

An imprint of Hodder Headline Limited

For more information about this series
and other Hodder Wayland titles, go to
www.hodderwayland.co.uk

Series concept: Ruth Thomson
Series Consultant: Erika Langmuir
Editor and Picture Research: Margot Richardson
Designers: Rachel Hamdi and Holly Mann

Copyright © Leo Thomson 2005

The right of Leo Thomson to be identified as the author of this
Work has been asserted by him in accordance with the
Copyright, Designs and Patents Act 1988.

British Library Cataloguing in Publication Data
Thomson, Leo
Place and Space: landscapes. - (Artventure)
1.Landscapes in art - Juvenile literature
2.Art appreciation - Juvenile literature
I.Title
704.9'436

ISBN 0 7502 45662

Printed in China

The publishers would like to thank the following for
permission to reproduce their pictures:
Page 1 © National Gallery Collection; By kind permission
of the Trustees of the National Gallery, London/CORBIS;
page 4 © Georgia O'Keeffe, ARS, NY and DACS, London 2003,
Provenance: Museo Thyssen-Bornemisza; page 5 © ADAGP,
Paris and DACS, London 2003, National Gallery of Art,
Washington DC, USA, Lauros /Giraudon /Bridgeman Art Library
/www.bridgeman.co.uk; page 6 Wallace Collection, London,
UK/www.bridgeman.co.uk; page 7 Tate, London 2004;
pages 8-9 © National Gallery Collection; By kind permission
of the Trustees of the National Gallery, London/CORBIS;
page 11 Alte Pinakothek, Munich, Germany, Lauros/Giraudon/
Bridgeman Art Library/ www.bridgeman.co.uk; page 12 L&M
Services BV Amsterdam 2004057; page 13 © 1986 David
Hockney/The J Paul Getty Museum, Los Angeles; page 14 ©
Burstein Collection/CORBIS; page 15 Tate, London 2004; pages
16-17 © Bettmann/CORBIS; pages 18-19 National Gallery,
London, UK/www.bridgeman.co.uk; page 20 © Francis G.
Mayer/CORBIS; page 21 Tate, London 2004; page 22 ©
Copyright of the Trustees of The British Museum; page 23
National Palace Museum, Taipei, Taiwan, Republic of China;
page 24 © Joseph Stella/Yale University Art Gallery (Gift of
Collection Societe Anonyme); page 25 © Tullio Crali, by kind
permission of Massimo Crali/Private Collection, Rome, Italy,
Credit: Accademia Italiana, London/www.bridgeman.co.uk;
page 26 The Zimmerman Family Collection, photo
© John Bigelow Taylor; page 27 © Jerry Uelsmann.

weblinks

For more information about
landscapes in art, go to
www.waylinks.co.uk/series/
artventure/landscape

Contents

Words in **bold** can be found in the glossary

Looking at landscapes

❑ Georgia O'Keeffe, **From the Plains II**, *1954*

Landscape is the space which surrounds us out of doors. It is where earth and sky, night and day, nature and people meet. Artists have pictured landscapes all over the world, at various times of day, in all weathers, and in every season. They have painted local scenes, faraway places and landscapes they see only in their dreams.

A window on the world

Artists share with us what they see, think and feel in the space of the landscape. A picture can **immerse** us in the **sensation** of a place. A landscape picture can be a window on to another world, making us think of being outside in nature, even when we are inside a building in a city.

4

A sense of place and space

Georgia O'Keeffe was a twentieth-century American artist. She lived in the New Mexican desert, and often painted outside in the wilderness. This painting captures her feeling of being in the vast, wild expanse of the American plains, under the fiery glow of the sunlit sky.

- How do you know when you are looking at a picture and not the real world?
- Which frames are landscape and which are portrait in the picture below?

Framing a scene

The shape of a picture frames the view we see in it. Pictures taller than wide are called 'portrait'. Pictures wider than tall are called 'landscape', although a picture of a landscape can be any shape.

Magritte was a Belgian painter who lived from 1898 to 1967. His painting has three **frames**: the edges of the canvas on the easel, the window frame, and the edges of the picture itself. Magritte makes us aware of the frames, letting us see the scene as if we were both inside and outside at the same time.

❑ René Magritte
The Human Condition
1933

5

The grand landscape

❏ Peter Paul Rubens, **Landscape with a Rainbow,** *1636*

Artists have often pictured people in the natural environment, to show our relationship to the earth.

Life on earth

Rubens, a **Flemish** artist, painted this **idyllic** scene showing people living in peace with the natural world, enjoying the fruits of the earth. On an autumn afternoon, with the sun low in the sky, farmers harvest the season's crops.

Rainbow of life

In the Bible, the rainbow after passing rain is a **symbol** of God's promise to let life flourish in its many different ways on earth. Here, the rainbow ties the colour and space of the picture together and guides our eye across the scene. We see the landscape spreading far into the distance, giving a sense of the **expanse** of the world.

□ John Martin
The Great Day of His Wrath
1851-53

▲ The scene is lit by the dramatic light of fire and lightning.

▲ A whole city is thrown into the air and falls back to earth.

▲ The land rises on each side, trapping us in the scene.

• What qualities make a landscape peaceful or terrifying?

• What differences in colour, light and **shape** can you see in these two pictures?

The end of the world

Here man is at the mercy of nature, as the earth spits fire, mountains crumble and lightning strikes. Martin, a nineteenth-century British painter, tells the story of the end of the world brought by God's anger at mankind. Martin uses the trembling figures in the **foreground** to show the terror of the situation and the awesome sense of **scale** of the scene.

Here I stand

It seems as if we could walk right into this picture and along the country road. We feel as if we are there, looking far into the distance, even though we are looking at a flat painting. The artist has created this **illusion** of space using the technique of **perspective**, a way of showing three-dimensional space in a flat picture.

❑ Meindert Hobbema, **The Avenue at Middleharnis**, *1689*

Flat space

The picture is like a window on to the scene, as if the rays of light seen through the window turned to paint on its surface. The space contained in the scene is flattened on to the **canvas**, so when we look at the picture the scene seems to spread out far behind the painting itself.

Deep space

The picture mimics the way we see the world. Objects further away appear smaller and smaller until they disappear into the distance. Things in the distance appear paler and less detailed, as if we were seeing them through miles of air.

- When you look around you, how do you know how far away things are?
- Why do things change in appearence as you move around them?

8

Our viewpoint

When we look at this picture, we see the scene from a particular **viewpoint**: the place our eyes would be to see the scene. Our viewpoint for this picture is as if we were standing in the middle of the road.

The horizon

The furthest we can see is the **horizon**, where earth and sky appear to meet. The horizon is as far as we can see round the curve of the earth.

The vanishing point

On the horizon, the sides of the road appear to meet and vanish. This is the **vanishing point** of the picture, the furthest we can see on the path. Everything in the picture shrinks in size towards this point.

◻ Meindert Hobbema, **The Avenue at Middleharnis**, *1689*

Time to meet

In the distance, a man with a dog is walking towards us. We know we will meet him eye to eye walking on the path, as his head appears in our line of sight. This creates an expectation of the future, pulling us into a journey along the avenue.

Window of time

Just looking at the picture we have no way of knowing whether the scene existed or not. We believe in it because it looks real. In fact, the picture is a very accurate **recreation** of a view in south Holland, that has hardly changed since Hobbema painted it in 1689. His artistic skill transports us to this distant time and place.

◀ The sky seems to slope down to the horizon.

◀ The trees shrink in size towards the vanishing point.

◀ The barn stretches towards the vanishing point.

◀ The horizon is low in the frame, making us feel close to the ground.

◀ The road narrows to the vanishing point.

- Why can't we see all the way around the earth?
- How different would things look if we had the viewpoint of a bird in the air?

A global perspective

A perspective view can connect the things we see close by with the wide expanse of the earth.

A changing world

This picture shows history in the making: the victory of the Greek leader, Alexander the Great, over the **Persians**, in 334BC. Altdorfer, a German artist working in the sixteenth century, set the battle within a vast landscape of earth, water and sky, to express this epic struggle and the battle's huge impact on the world.

A cosmic view

The picture uses an all-embracing perspective to connect people, mountains, sea and sky. Our bird's-eye view rises from the action of the battle in the foreground up into the air, revealing more and more landscape, until we see the curve of the earth itself.

Universal time

The picture captures more than an **instant** of time. We see the sun and the moon, day and night together. On the ground below, the **chaos** of battle stretches through days and nights.

A world in the eye

The picture creates a whole world for our eyes to roam in, following the great detail of the scene. The vertical frame emphasizes the connection between earth and sky, revealing the worlds of both humans and the heavens at once.

Time of life

Altdorfer was an architect and a politician as well as a painter. He declined the post of mayor in his town, Regensburg, so as to have time to complete this monumental painting.

The life of a painting

The painting only became famous hundreds of years after it was painted. In 1800, Napoleon's army carried it from Munich to Paris, where Napoleon is said to have kept it in his bathroom. It was later exhibited in the Louvre in Paris and has now finally returned to Munich.

- How high would we have to fly to see the whole earth at once?
- Is it unusual to see the sun and the moon together in the sky?

The clouds seem to part for the tablet recording the battle.

The tassel points to Alexander chasing Darius, the Persian leader, who flees on his chariot.

The battle is lit up by the dramatic red glow of the sunset.

The horizon is high in the picture, making us feel high up in the air.

The swarms of soldiers guide our eye around the scene.

At the bottom of the picture we are near the ground and feel close to the action.

❑ Albrecht Altdorfer
Battle of Issus, *1529*
Issus was an ancient town in Asia Minor, where Turkey is today.

Multiple perspectives

Pa Tour 1910

r delaunay 19

When we are in a space, we move our eyes to see in all directions, and walk about to get different viewpoints. A picture with a single, **static** viewpoint cannot capture all these movements.

All at once

Cubism is a way of painting with multiple viewpoints, all shown at the same time, capturing a scene from all angles, giving a sense of motion in time. This painting shows the Eiffel Tower in Paris, as seen both from the ground upwards and from a dizzying height in the clouds. There is no horizon or vanishing point, so we feel as if we are floating in space.

❏ Robert Delaunay
Tour Eiffel 1910 (Eiffel Tower)
1911
In 1911, Paris was centre of the artistic world and the Eiffel Tower its symbol of modern city life and technological skill.

❑ David Hockney
**Pearlblossom Hwy.,
11-18th April, 1986 #2**
1986

A wandering viewpoint

Hockney is a contemporary artist who is interested in art that takes time to make and time to look at. He spent nine days walking around the desert in California, USA, taking photographs from different viewpoints, some low down and some from the top of a ladder. Hockney had the photos printed at his local photo lab, then spent two weeks in his studio carefully composing more than 500 of them into this **collage**. The result is a record of his time spent indoors as well as outdoors in the landscape. The finished picture looks as if it had one central viewpoint. In fact, it has many, creating a view you could never see in real life.

• Why does it take time to experience space?

Texture of the elements

Landscape is made of natural **elements**: earth, water, fire, air and space. But pictures are made of paint, ink or other materials. Artists use these materials to recreate nature's qualities in their work, using their own language of colour, **texture** and **form**.

Calm storm

The Japanese artist, Hokusai, sets a violent storm against the quiet mass of Mount Fuji. He freezes the moment of a lightning strike with sharp, **abstract** shapes. In the distance, the coloured tones of earth, water and sky blend to evoke the drifting, storm filled air.

❏ Hokusai
Mount Fuji Above the Lightning
1829-33

The picture is a woodcut print, made by carefully cutting out lines in a block of wood, then inking the block to print on paper. This is an ancient technique used to make thousands of pictures from a single drawing.

Storm of paint

In this painting by Turner, a British artist, the paint *is* the storm. The paint blows like the wind, washes like the sea and drives like the snow. Turner claimed that he was tied to the mast of a ship to experience the storm. He recreated the movement and energy of the storm on the canvas, mixing his paint into the continuous whirl of water moving between sea and sky. All we see is water. There is no horizon and our view is tilted as if we are aboard the swaying ship.

- What makes water look wet?
- Could you draw water with any materials you liked?

❏ JMW Turner
Snowstorm: Steamboat off a Harbour's Mouth
1842

Earthly paradise

A picture can evoke the atmosphere of a time and place, whether real or **imaginary**.

Urban paradise

Here Seurat, a French artist, pictures the river Seine in Paris as an earthly paradise. Nature provides a gentle and peaceful place of leisure. The Parisiens simply gaze upon the world. The day shimmers with the heat and colour of summer and the vitality of nature fills every inch of the canvas. The surface is carefully painted with an **intricate** pattern of colour, suggesting the endless variety of natural forms.

▲ Long shadows suggest the afternoon sun.

▲ The people have glowing haloes of light around their heads.

▲ Dark shadowy areas make the sunlit areas seem brighter.

▲ The dog is frozen in mid-leap, capturing the stillness of an instant.

❑ George Seurat **Sunday Afternoon on the Island of La Grande Jatte,** *1884-86*

Particles of colour

Seurat painted with millions of individual dots of colour. He invented this technique, called pointillism, based on the scientific theory of his time. The dots of colour mix in the eye when seen from a distance, but keep their own individual brilliance.

Complementary colours

Pairs of complementary colours placed together look more brilliant than colours on their own. Seurat used a version of a colour wheel (see above, top right) to calculate which colours are complementary and placed these next to each other on the canvas, creating millions of colour contrasts in the scene.

Colour of time

The painting has the warm orange glow of a summer's afternoon. Everything has both its own colour and specks of colour of the things around it. Seurat added tiny specs of orange for the sunlight falling on the scene.

green   yellow

cyan   red

blue   magenta

Colour wheel

Seurat used tiny dots of complementary colours to create a vivid and brilliant effect.

❏ George Seurat
Sunday Afternoon on the Island of La Grande Jatte, 1884-86
(detail)

◀ Today we know that the human eye can see more than 7 million different colours. Artists can mix most of these from just three **primary colours**: cyan, magenta and yellow.

◀ Pairs of colours opposite each other on the wheel are complementary colours: yellow and blue, red and cyan, magenta and green. Any two complementary colours mixed together will make dull, greyish tones, but put side by side they seem dazzlingly bright.

An ideal moment

This painting occupied Seurat for almost two years. He visited the island every day for months, making studies of the landscape. He also had models pose in his studio. He put all these together to create an imaginary moment in time.

An eternal instant

The picture forms a world of delicate **harmony** and variety, the fleeting qualities of an instant. Seurat gives the moment such grandeur that it lasts in the mind, like a memory, taking on a life of its own.

Wild vision

☐ Vincent van Gogh
Cornfield with Cypresses
1889

▲ Complementary blues and yellows give the scene a heat-struck intensity.

▲ The shrubs in the foreground give a sense of depth to the field.

▲ The tall cypress trees, associated with cemeteries and death, are dark figures in the scene.

❏ Vincent van Gogh
Cornfield with Cypresses (detail)
The clouds are painted with thick brush strokes giving a sense of their bulk and weight compared to the thin blue sky.

Our state of mind changes the way we see the world. A picture can give shape to an artist's thoughts and moods, sharing with us his or her unique vision of life.

Nature of the mind

In this picture, the Dutch painter, Vincent van Gogh, captures the ever-changing energy of nature. He gives everything a wild and shifting form. Each brush stroke is thick and distinct, giving weight and volume to the forms of plants, rock and sky. Every mark is different, shaped by the changing flow of Van Gogh's thoughts.

Colour in a tube

The **vivid** colours of the painting come from the bright ready-made paints which Van Gogh's brother regularly posted to him from Paris. These newly invented paints let Van Gogh work quickly, on his own and out of doors without having to worry about mixing his colours from **pigments**.

Fragile nature

Van Gogh saw the world with extreme intensity and pictured it so. He was often mentally unstable and is famous for cutting off his earlobe in a mad fit.

He continued to paint even when admitted to hospital for mental illness. This picture was painted near the hospital in St-Rémy-de-Provence, France, where he spent a year at the end of his life.

• Do any two clouds in the sky ever take exactly the same shape?

❏ Vincnet van Gogh
Cornfield with Cypresses (detail)
The wheat is painted with very thick paint, like a layer of tiny sculptures on the canvas.

Scenes and stories

A landscape can tell a story, **evoking** the past, present and future of a scene all at the same time.

Fateful future

This picture is like a moment in a film: we wonder what will happen next. The forces of nature have created the drama. The wind and the waves have wrecked the boat's mast and sails, leaving it drifting on the currents. Now hungry sharks circle the boat. There is blood in the water and a **tornado** looms on the horizon, threatening the lone sailor with death. We cannot be sure whether the tornado will pass, or if the ship in the distance might come to the rescue. We are left to watch the sailor think about his uncertain future.

☐ Winslow Homer, **The Gulf Stream**, *1889*

❏ Paul Nash, **We are Making a New World**, *1918*

Silent land

Paul Nash was a British soldier and war artist in the First World War. He **sketched** this scene of devastation on the front line in France and painted it on his return to England. The scene is empty of people, suggesting a battle with no survivors.

The landscape itself tells the story. The sun passes behind red clouds, suggesting the blood of war. The land has been churned up by battle and the trees are burned to their cores. However, the sun is perhaps a symbol of hope in the scene as it still rises and sets and the cycles of life go on.

Slow landscapes

Natural form changes all the time. Looking closely, we can become lost in its details.

War and peace

This scene, part of a book painted by Sultan Muhammad in Persia in the sixteenth century, pictures the hero, Rustam, asleep in the forest while his horse battles a lion. The warrior rests at peace, surrounded by the lush beauty of the forest. A rich patchwork of colours and styles captures the variety of life. The clouds twirl and even the rocks seem alive. The scene just piles up, without any strict perspective, giving everything a strange scale. The free **composition** and loose borders let the individual parts flourish and the text float through the scene.

❑ Sultan Muhammad (attributed to)
**Rustam Sleeps while Rakhsh Fights
Off a Lion**
1515-22

Timeless space

Fan Kuan, an eleventh-century artist, lived in the mountains of Shansi in China. His picture takes our eyes on a journey through the landscape, following the path as it climbs up the mountains from the valley. We see far more of the landscape than we could ever see at one time from any one viewpoint. Misty clouds hide the path and the horizon, suggesting an unknown space and time between the mountains. The scene has been left unfinished, letting us complete the landscape and our journey in our mind.

• Can a picture ever really be complete and totally describe all of a landscape?

❏ Fan Kuan
Scholar Pavilion in the Cloudy Mountain, Song Dynasty
11th Century

Fast landscapes

Joseph Stella
**Battle of Lights,
Coney Island, Mardi Gras**
1913-14

▲ The shapes and colours pile up, like hundreds of sensations felt at once.

▲ The **silhouettes** of dancers blend with abstract forms to make a writhing sea of life.

▲ The steel girders of the rollercoaster rides tangle up with all the action.

Our **technology** changes the landscape. We make the world bright with electric lights, noisy with speeding cars and planes, and warmer with all our activity. Artists have expressed this **frantic** modern landscape with intense, **dynamic** images.

Speeding space

Joseph Stella, an Italian-American, painting in the early twentieth century, depicts a man-made landscape throbbing with electricity (left). The lights, noise and speed of the carnival collapse into a whirl of shape and colour. There is no single moment in time or viewpoint in space. All the sensations of the night come together in a seething mass of rhythm and form, to make an abstract modern world.

- How does electricity change our landscape?
- How does a scene look different viewed from a moving car or plane?

❏ Tullio Crali
Dogfight
1936-38

Spinning world

The painting above captures the sweeping, curling path of a plane in a single speeding image. The ground spins as we loop the loop with the pilot. The plane's movement warps his view of the earth, curving the horizon and turning the world upside-down.

Landscapes of the mind

Artists can use the elements of landscape to portray fantastical visions of strange, alternative realities.

Inner worlds

This picture is a mandala, a **diagram** made by **Buddhists**, to picture the inner forces of the **universe**. It expresses the connection between the inner world of the mind and the outer world of our environment.

Order and chaos

At the centre is a small triangle of calm with a symbol of a goddess, surrounded by a terrifying world of blood and fire. The man-made shapes of the square, circle and triangle contrast with the wild forms of the seething ocean and raging flames.

The world seems balanced between order and chaos, each existing within the other.

▲ The blue triangle seems to float in an endless universe of fire.

▲ The human figure forms a whole continent in the middle of a red ocean. Within his body is an inner mandala of **symmetrical** forms.

❑ Unknown artist
Geluk Order, Tibet
Fire Mandala
17th-18th century

Try placing a mirror along the centre line to see how the image is symmetrical.

◀ The trees float free of gravity, as if on another planet.

◀ The tree roots are a photograph of a leafless winter tree turned upside-down. The combined tree has both its summer and winter form.

◀ The seed pod is a symbol of natural reproduction and the cycles of birth and death.

❏ Jerry Uelsmann, **Floating Tree**, *1969*

Human nature

This photograph plays with nature to create an unearthly **reality**. The land on the left is a mirror image of the one on the right and two identical trees float above the scene, their roots free of the earth. The artist pictures a strange, intelligent nature dividing and multipliying to reproduce itself.

Uelsmann, an American artist, took photos of real landscape and played with these in the **darkroom**, carefully combining many images to make a a single print. He does not use computers to alter images, preferring the mystery of darkness and chemical reactions. He creates a nature of the mind, exploring the mysterious workings of the world and our thoughts.

About the artists

The symbols below show the size and shape of the works shown in this book, compared to an average-sized adult.

Albrecht ALTDORFER (pages 10-11)
(1480-1538) German
Battle of Issus, 1529
Oil on panel, 158 x 120 cm
Alte Pinakothek, Munich, Germany

Other landscapes
❑ *Landscape with Castle*, 1522-25
   Alte Pinakothek, Munich, Germany
❑ *Willow Landscape*, 1511
   Akedemie der Bildenden Kunste, Vienna, Austria

Tullio CRALI (page 25)
(1910-2000) Italian
Dogfight I, 1936-38
Oil on board, 100 x 110 cm
Private Collection

Other landscapes
❑ *Nose Dive on the City*, 1939
   Private Collection
❑ *The Force of the Curve*, 1930
   Private Collection
❑ *Ostacolista*, 1930
   Private Collection

Robert DELAUNAY (page 12)
(1885-1941) French
Eiffel Tower, 1911
Oil on canvas, 201.9 x 138.4 cm
Solomon R. Guggenheim Museum, New York, USA

Other landscapes
❑ *Circular Forms*, 1930
   Solomon R. Guggenheim Museum, New York, USA
❑ *Simultaneous Contrasts: Sun and Moon*, 1913
   The Museum of Modern Art, New York, USA

Vincent van GOGH (pages 18-19)
(1853-1890) Dutch
Cornfield with Cypresses, 1889
Oil on Canvas, 72.5 x 91.5 cm
National Gallery, London, UK

Other landscapes
❑ *Starry Night*, 1889
   Metropolitan Museum of Art, New York, USA
❑ *Field Under Thunderclouds*, 1890
   Vincent van Gogh Foundation, Amsterdam, Holland

Meindert HOBBEMA (pages 8-9)
(1638-1709) Dutch
The Avenue at Middleharnis, 1689
Oil on canvas, 103.5 x 141 cm
The National Gallery, London, UK

Other landscapes
❑ *Woodland Road*, 1670
   The Metropolitan Museum of Art, New York, USA
❑ *A Wooded Landscape*, 1667
   J Paul Getty Museum, Los Angeles, CA, USA

David HOCKNEY (page 13)
(1937-) British
Pearlblossom Hwy., 11-18th April, 1986, #2, 1986
Photographic collage, 198 x 282 cm
The J. Paul Getty Museum, Los Angeles, CA, USA

Other landscapes
❑ *A Walk Around the Hotel Courtyard, Acatlan*, 1985
   Andre Emmerich Gallery, New York, USA
❑ *The Brooklyn Bridge*, 1982
   Private collection

HOKUSAI (page 14)
(1760-1849) Japanese
Mount Fuji Above the Lightning, 1829-33
Woodcut print, 25.9 x 38.2 cm
Musée Guimet, Paris, France

Other landscapes
- ❑ *The Great Wave off Kanagawa*, 1830-31
  The Metropolitan Museum of Art, New York, USA
- ❑ *A Sudden Gust of Wind at Ejri*, 1831
  Musée Guimet, Paris, France

Winslow HOMER (page 20)

(1836-1910) American
The Gulf Stream, 1889
Oil on canvas, 71.4 x 124.8 cm
The Metropolitan Museum of Art, New York, USA

Other landscapes
- ❑ *Moonlight, Wood Island Night*, 1894
  The Metropolitan Museum of Art, New York, USA
- ❑ *A Summer Night*, 1890
  Palais de Alma, Paris, France
- ❑ *Kissing the Moon*, 1904
  Addison Gallery of American Art, MASS, USA

Fan KUAN (page 23)
(Active 10th-early 11th Century) Chinese
Scholar Pavillon in the Cloudy Mountain, Song Dynasty,
11th Century
Ink on Silk
National Palace Museum, Taipei, Taiwan, Republic of China

Other landscapes
- ❑ *Travellers Among Mountains and Streams*, 11th Century
  National Palace Museum, Taipei, Taiwan, Republic of China
- ❑ *Winter Landscape with Temples and Travelers*, 11th
  Century, Museum of Fine Arts, Boston, MASS, USA

René MAGRITTE (page 5)

(1898-1967) Belgian
The Human Condition, 1933
Oil on Canvas, 80.7 x 100.6 cm
Private Collection

Other landscapes
- ❑ *Golconda*, 1953, Private collection
- ❑ *The Empire of Lights*, 1958, Private Collection
- ❑ *Free hand*, 1965
  National Gallery of Art, Washington DC, USA

John MARTIN (page 7)

(1789-1854) British
The Great Day of His Wrath,
1851-53
Oil on Canvas, 196.5 x 303.2 cm
Tate Britain, London, UK

Other landscapes
- ❑ *The Last Judgement*, 1853
  Tate Britain, London, UK
- ❑ *The Plains of Heaven*, 1853
  Tate Britain, London, UK

Sultan MUHAMMAD (attributed to, page 22)

(15th-16th Century) Iranian (Tabriz)
Rustam Sleeps while Rakhsh Fights Off a Lion,
1515-22
Page from a manuscript of the Shahnama
(Book of Kings), Gouache on paper, 40.8 x 29.3 cm
British Museum, London, UK

Other landscapes
- ❑ *The Court of Gayumars*, from The Shah Tahmasp
  Shamana of Firdausi, 1522-25
  Collection of Prince and Princess Sadruddin Aga Kahn
- ❑ Pages from *Gulistan of Sa'di*, 1525-30
  Keir Collection

Paul NASH (page 21)
(1889-1946) British
We Are Making a New World, 1918
Oil on Canvas, 71.4 x 91.4 cm
Imperial War Museum, London, UK

Other landscapes
- ❑ *The Menin Road*, 1918-19
  Imperial War Museum, London, UK
- ❑ *Totes Meer*, 1940-41, Tate Britain, London, UK

Georgia O'KEEFFE (page 4)

(1887-1986) American
From the Plains II, 1954
Oil on Canvas, 122 x 183 cm
Fundación Colleción Thyssen-Bornemisza, Madrid, Spain

Other works

☐ *Winter Road I*, 1963,
National Gallery of Art, Washington DC, USA
☐ *Sky Above the Clouds I*, 1963
The Georgia O'Keeffe Museum, Santa Fe, New Mexico, USA
☐ *Summer Days*, 1936
Whitney Museum of American Art, New York, USA

Peter Paul RUBENS (page 6)

(1577-1640) Flemish
Landscape with a Rainbow, 1636
Oil on oak, 136 x 235 cm
Wallace Collection, London, UK

Other landscapes

☐ *An Autumn Landscape with a View of Het Steen in the Morning*, 1636
National Gallery, London, UK
☐ *Stormy Landscape with Pilemon Baucis*, 1627
Kunsthistorisches Museum, Vienna, Austria

Georges SEURAT (pages 16-17)

(1851-1891) French
Sunday Afternoon on the Island of La Grande Jatte, 1884-86
Oil on Canvas, 207.6 x 308 cm
The Art Institute of Chicago, Chicago, ILL, USA

Other landscapes

☐ *Bathers at Asnières*, 1883-84
National Gallery, London, UK
☐ *La Bec Du Hoc Grandcamp*, 1885
Tate Britain, London, UK
☐ *Channel at Gravelines, Petit Fort Phillipe*, 1890
Indianapolis Museum of Art, IN, USA

Joseph STELLA (page 24)

(1877-1946) Italian
Battle of Lights, Coney Island, Mardi Gras, 1913-14
Oil on Canvas, 195.3 x 214.9 cm
Yale University Art Gallery, New Haven, CT, USA

Other landscapes

☐ *Flowers, Italy*, 1930, Phoenix Art Museum, USA
☐ *Tree of My Life*, 1919-20
Mr and Mrs Barney A Ebsworth Foundation and Windsor Inc, St Louis, MISS, USA
☐ *New York Interpreted (The Voice of the City)*, 1920-22
The Newark Museum, New Jersey, USA

JMW TURNER (page 15)

(1775-1851) British
Snowstorm: Steamboat off a Harbour's Mouth, 1842
Oil on Canvas, 91.4 x 121.9 cm
Tate Britain, London, UK

Other landscapes

☐ *Hannibal and His Army Crossing The Alps*, 1812
Tate Britain, London, UK
☐ *Light and Colour, Goethes Theory – The Morning After the Deluge*, 1843, Tate Liverpool, Liverpool, UK

Jerry UELSMANN (page 27)

(1934-) American
Floating Tree, 1969
Gelatin Siver print, 40 x 50 cm
Collection of Jerry Uelsmann

Unknown artist: Geluk Order, Tibet (page 26)

Fire Mandala, 17th-18th century
Ink and watercolours on cloth, 61 x 47 cm
The Zimmerman Family Collection, New York, USA

Other Buddhist mandalas

☐ *Kalachakra Mandala*, 17th Century
Museum of Fine Arts, Boston, MASS, USA
☐ *Mandala of Six Chakravartins*, 15th Century
Philadelphia Museum of Art, Philadelphia, PA, USA

Glossary

Abstract Shapes and forms not shown in a real way.

Buddhist A person who follows Buddhism, a religion from India.

Canvas A piece of coarse, stretched cloth on which most oil paintings are done.

Chaos Complete disorder and confusion.

Collage An artwork made of lots of pieces stuck together.

Composition An arrangement of shape, form and space.

Darkroom A completely darkened room for developing film and photographs.

Diagram A simplified drawing that shows how things work.

Dynamic Full of energy, movement or change.

Elements Basic parts.

Evoking Calling up in the mind.

Expanse A wide stretch.

Flemish From Flanders, a place that is now divided between Belgium, France and the Netherlands.

Foreground The part of a painting that seems closest to the viewer.

Form The complete three-dimensional shape of an object.

Frame A border around something.

Frantic Fast and chaotic.

Harmony A complete and balanced state.

Horizon The line where the earth's surface and the sky appear to meet.

Idyllic Blissful or peaceful.

Illusion A false or unreal picture, idea or belief.

Imaginary Something only in the mind.

Immerse Put in completely.

Instant A particular moment of time.

Intricate Finely detailed.

Persians People from a place called Persia (now known as Iran).

Perspective A method of painting or drawing landscapes, figures and objects to make them appear three-dimensional.

Pigments The colours in paint.

Primary colours Cyan, magenta and yellow (often confused with blue, red and yellow); pure colours that cannot be made by mixing any colours together.

Recreation Creating something again.

Reality What is real.

Scale The relative size of things.

Sensation A feeling our senses give us.

Shape The form or outline of someone or something.

Silhouettes A shape or form shown only as an outline.

Sketched Drew quickly or roughly. (Sketches are often done as a guide for a more detailed painting.)

Static Without movement, action or change.

Symbol Something that stands for something else.

Symmetrical Made of parts that are a mirror image of each other.

Technology The use of science for practical purposes.

Texture The feel and appearance of a surface.

Tornado A funnel-shaped cloud made by violently circling winds.

Universe Everything that exists.

Vanishing point The point at which parallel lines going back appear to join together in the distance.

Viewpoint The place our eyes would be to see a scene in a painting or other work of art.

Vivid Intensely deep or bright.

Index